Larne

and the

Road to the Glens

An Illustrated History and Companion

Paintings by
Sam McLarnon U.W.S

Text by
Felix McKillop

Cottage
Publications

First published by Cottage Publications,
Donaghadee N. Ireland 1995.
Copyrights Reserved
© Illustrations by Sam McLarnon 1995
© Text by Felix McKillop 1995
All rights reserved.
Printed in Singapore

ISBN 0 9516402 9 1

List of Contents

The Artist

Born in Larne where he still lives, Sam McLarnon has been painting on the coast of Antrim for many years in his favourite medium of watercolour. Indeed rare would be the day, rain, hail or shine, when Sam cannot be found somewhere in the Glens with his paints and easel.

From his student days he holds six gold, silver and bronze awards as well as a diploma in illustration. He has long been a member of the Ulster Watercolour Society and his distinctive style is highly valued both at home and abroad as witnessed by the demand for his previous book in this series, 'Ballycastle and the Heart of the Glens'.

The Author

Born and still living in the Glenarm area with his wife Janie, and two young children, Michelle and Catherine, Felix is a teacher at St. Comgall's High School, Larne where he is head of the Geography Department. He has always taken a keen interest in the history of the local area, particularly in its genealogy and that element of history which is passed down by word of mouth and is thus in danger of being forgotten. In 1987 he published 'Glenarm, a Local History' an historical record of his native area which proved very popular with both the local population and visitors to the area. He is currently researching a history of Glencloy and Carnlough which is due for publication in 1996.

Larne and Other Parts

The Glens of Antrim stretch from a few miles north of Larne to Ballycastle on the northern coast. Due to their inaccessibility they remained isolated and virtually cut off from the rest of the country until the 19th century. Such was the isolation that it became easier for inhabitants in the middle Glens to trade over the channel with Scotland rather than towns like Carrickfergus and Belfast. All that changed in the early 19th century with the building of the Grand Military Way, more popularly known as the Antrim Coast Road. For the first time the area was open to the masses and many people travelled from the rest of the country, as well as England and Scotland, to see the exquisite natural beauty of the area. The port of Larne, being only a short sea journey from Scotland, was a natural entrance for tourists from Britain. Larne quickly gained the reputation of being the 'Gateway to the Glens'.

People have been settling along this part of the Antrim Coast for over 5000 years. Excavations carried out in 1935 by archaeologists from Harvard University (USA) uncovered no fewer than 10000 flints, shaped for use as knives, scrapers and perforators, along Curran Point (originally 'Corran' from the Gaelic word for sickle) in Larne. This find showed that people had settled here around 3000 B.C. So important was the discovery in archaeological terms that this period in Ireland is often referred to as the 'Larnian Culture'. Excavations carried out by the same team of archaeologists at Cloney, Glenarm, also unearthed vast quantities of Stone Age flint implements of a similar period.

The earliest peoples who settled in the area were tribes who wandered northward across Europe before eventually crossing the 30 miles or so over the Irish Sea on primitive boats to reach Ireland. It is likely that the valleys and hills at that time would have been covered in dense forests which would have been the natural habitat for deer, wild pigs, wolves and other smaller animals like the hare. The people who lived on the Curran at Larne were primitive hunters who killed for their food and used the flints as scrapers to clean the animal hides afterwards.

The hills above Larne, Glenarm and Carnlough still yield evidence of ancient settlement. Standing stones, burial chambers and 'Giants' Graves', a legacy of a prehistoric culture, are found hidden away in the less fertile, inaccessible areas of the hills. The pagan settlers cremated their dead. The ashes of more important members of these early settler groups were put into clay urns and placed on the ground surrounded by layers of stones and soil. Some of the burial mounds were very elaborate and quite large. Many consisted of large stones placed on their end (with a cap stone sitting on top) surrounded by smaller stones and then finished with a soil covering. Burial chambers dating back to 3000 BC and beyond can be seen today at Ticloy above Glencloy, Gowkstown and Dunteige in the hills above Glenarm and Cloughogan in Cairncastle. Many of these graves were used by families and as they were so large it was assumed by later inhabitants, who had no memory of earlier generations, that they were giants' graves.

In the century before the Christian era, the King of Ireland was known as Hugony the Great. He was said to have had 22 sons and 3 daughters. To one of his sons, Lathar, he gave the area along the Antrim coast from about Glenarm to the Inver River at Larne. This area became known as 'the district of Lathar' - in Gaelic 'Latharna' from which the name Larne is derived.

The Larne area was also known much further afield, though not necessarily by this name. The famous Greek geographer Ptolemy knew about Islandmagee and mentioned it in a geographical account written early in the 2nd century. This piece of land which shelters

Larne Lough was shown on his maps as 'Isamnion Akron'. Also as far back as 205 A.D. the Roman Emperor Serverus wrote describing how a Roman galley with its captain, Virgilius Collatinus, had been blown off course after leaving the Solway Firth and had taken shelter in the area of water we know today as Larne Lough. While awaiting repairs to his storm-damaged vessel, the captain had heard from the locals of an ancient settlement which once had existed there but which had disappeared long since. Obviously the settlement was revived as succeeding generations saw the natural advantages of the area around Larne Lough and the Curran. As you look down on Larne Lough from the Cairncastle Road today, it is easy to picture the flat land around the lough stretching backwards inland and rising sharply towards Craigyhill and Inver. The Inver River and its tributary the Naggy Burn provided fresh water for the early settlers.

The Christianisation of Ireland is often credited to St. Patrick though there were missionaries here before him. The story is well known of his slavery at Slemish near Broughshane, his escape and later return as a bishop. Ancient churches at the Glore near Glenarm, St. Cunning in Cairncastle and the old church at Glynn are said to be have been built by him. In his book 'In Praise of Ulster' Richard Hayward refers to a local tradition which states that St. Patrick crossed Larne Lough in a coracle and afterwards blessed it, saying that no lives would ever be lost crossing the lough. The story is unlikely to have any basis in fact and certainly lives have been lost over the years in the waters of the lough.

There are legends of St. Patrick's followers, St. McKenna and St. MacNissi, being associated with Ardclinis Church, the ruins of which can be seen today between Garron Point and Glenariff, but the presence of St. Comgall in Magheramorne, south of Larne, has greater substance in fact. Comgall was born at Magheramorne in 517, the son of a Pictish warrior, Setna, of the kingdom of Dal-Araidhe. This kingdom included most of southern County Antrim while Dalriada extended northward from Larne to the River Bush at Coleraine and included the Glens of Antrim. Comgall founded a monastery at Bangor between 552 and 559. This monastery became an important seat of learning, bringing student monks from all over Europe and at its height accommodating 3000 monks under the guidance of St. Comgall. Some authorities attribute his father's name, Setna, as being the same as Cedma and it is this name which lives on today in the church at Inver called St. Cedma's.

From the 8th to the 11th centuries the coasts around Ireland were invaded by marauders from Scandinavia. The Vikings with their longboats used Larne Lough, which resembled their own sheltered fjords in Scandinavia, as a base to launch attacks on the people here. These invaders referred to the lough as Ulfried's Fiord (Ulfried's Harbour) although over the years it was named Wal-frich-fiord, Walderfrith, Walverfleete, Udlefleet and eventually Olderfleet in the reign of Queen Elizabeth I. The 'fleet' in Olderfleet is a corruption of the Scandinavian fiord - 'an inlet of the sea'. The famous historian Reeves felt that in the first part of these various place names was disguised the ancient Irish name of the Larne or Inver river, viz. Ollarbha (or Ollarva) and that they were all imperfect attempts at representing the sound of Ollarbha fiord - the inlet into the sea into which the Ollarbha flows. Whatever the name, a famous naval battle took place in Larne Lough in 1018 between armies led by a Viking chief and the King of Ireland. The Viking, Einar Jarl, son of Sigurd, Earl of the Orkneys, was defeated by Konofogor (Connor), King of Ireland in the 'Bay of Ulpeksfiord' (Olderfleete). A skeleton, thought to be a Viking soldier from this battle, was found along the shore at Larne in 1840.

Olderfleet Castle, the ruins of which stand today on Curran Point a few yards north of the excavations carried out in 1935, is said to be of Danish origin though some sources suggest it was built by a Scottish family called Bisset around 1250. Certainly the Bissets lived in it at this time though it was probably built at an earlier date by the Viking invaders attempting to fortify an important point of entry for them. The castle was, some years ago, designated as an ancient monument by the government and will be preserved for future generations. In 1014 the Vikings suffered a major defeat at the hands of the army of Brian Boru, the Irish High King (Ard-Ri) at Clontarf near Dublin. As the defeated invaders retreated northward their last stronghold was said to be Dungallon, a great earthen fort on a hill near Carnlough.

A strange story concerning the last of the Vikings survives in oral tradition in the Glens. Apparently when the Danish power was broken in the north an old man and his son were the last of the Vikings left in that part of Ireland. As they fled they took refuge at Garron Point. Both apparently held a much sought secret, namely that they knew how to manufacture beer from heather. When they were captured by their enemies they were promised that their lives would be saved if they divulged their secret brew recipe. Determined to keep his secret, the father said he would only tell the recipe after his son was killed. When his wishes were granted he offered his own head to the sword stating that the secret would go with him.

Ireland was not the only country invaded by the Vikings. They pillaged most of the coastal areas of Europe. Many of them settled in areas that they had earlier invaded, including an area in France later known as Normandy. Years passed and the inhabitants of this region began to look for greener pastures. The Normans, as they were known, invaded and conquered England in 1066. Over a century later in 1169 the Normans came to Ireland and although they did not capture all of it their presence was felt as far north as Glenarm. Mottes, fortified natural or man-made mounds of earth which they used to consolidate their conquered areas, can be found in Cairncastle and Mullaghsandal. On top of these mounds of gravel and earth they built strong wooden forts which allowed them protection and a means of warding off attackers. There is a tradition that in the early 13th century the Anglo-Norman ruler in England, King John (1199-1216) really put Glenarm on the map when he granted a municipal charter to Glenarm giving it a corporation and making it perhaps the oldest town in Ulster. Certainly in later years the Earls of Antrim held manorial courts in the village and it was an important administrative and religious centre.

The Bisset family were said to have built a castle in Glenarm around 1270. This castle was partially pulled down in 1597 and a manor courthouse was later erected on its site. The Baptist Church presently holds services in this old building. Some years ago when repair work was being carried out on the courthouse a skeleton was discovered behind an old wall.

During the 14th century various clans in Ulster were fighting each other and it was common for soldiers called gallowglasses to come over from Scotland to fight for whatever clan would pay them the most. John Mor McDonnell, from the Western Isles of Scotland, came here to fight for the O'Neill clan. During his time here he met and, in 1399, married Margery Bisset who was one of the Bissets from Glenarm Castle. From this union came the McDonnell lineage who were later to become the Earls of Antrim.

When Edward Bruce and his Scottish army landed at Larne on 25th May, 1315 with 6000 troops in an attempt to make Bruce King of Ireland the most prominent building in sight was certainly Olderfleet Castle. The Bissett family who occupied the castle were obviously no match for such a large army and history records that the Bruce army was well received by the Bissets at Olderfleet Castle before setting out to engage the Anglo-Norman forces based at Carrickfergus. On their way Bruce's army was met by a large force of Anglo-Norman troops and a battle took place in which the Anglo-Normans were defeated and had to retreat back to Carrickfergus.

The place where this battle took place is said to be at Mounthill where a cairn of stones marked the scene of the engagement for many centuries. Bruce's army then set out to engage the McQuillan clan of North Antrim who aided the Anglo-Normans. A battle is said to have taken place at a steep hill called the 'Path' between Cairncastle and Glenarm. This tradition is supported by the discovery of vast quantities of human and horse bones in the early 19th century by a farmer who was digging a drain on a farm in the nearby townland of Solar. The successful Scottish armies headed towards the town of Connor (near Ballymena) to attack it but were again confronted by the McQuillans at a place now known as Carnalbanagh (the 'cairn of the Scots men') where a stone cairn lay for many years marking the scene of the skirmish. Bruce's invasion plans continued, winning some battles and losing others but in 1327 he signed a treaty with Sir Henry de Mandeville, seneschal of Ulster, and returned to Scotland. Thus, despite their pragmatism, the poor Bissets were to lose out anyway for it is said that as a result of having fought on Bruce's side that they later lost ownership of Olderfleet Castle.

In the 13th century a friary run by Premonstratensian monks, or White Canons, was built at Drumalis near Larne Harbour. It was possibly founded by the Bissets who may also have been responsible for the founding of a Franciscan monastery around 1470 in Glenarm. The latter was run by the Friars of the Third Order of St. Francis. The remains of the Glenarm monastery can be seen today in the graveyard beside the Church of Ireland. When the final order was issued by Henry VIII for the dissolution of the Irish monasteries in 1542, the last abbot of Woodburn handed over to the King's Commissioners his priory at Woodburn including that at 'Clondumalis' (Drumalis). The fate of the monastery at Glenarm was probably the same as records show that it was used as a barracks by Queen Elizabeth's soldiers in 1568.

In 1568 Sir Moses Hill came to Ulster from England and was later made Governor of Olderfleet Castle by Queen Elizabeth I in order to defend the country against the Scots. Hill lived a good deal at Olderfleet Castle and he strengthened and repaired it as well as raising earthworks around it. An army, under the leadership of Moses Hill and Sir John Chichester, fought a battle with the McDonnells of the Glens of Antrim at Aldfracken in Templecorran. The McDonnells won the battle and Sir John lost his life. Moses Hill fled the battle scene and headed for Olderfleet Castle hotly pursued by the McDonnells. Hill's land retreat was cut off on the Corran Peninsula by the McDonnells and he escaped with his life by swimming his horse across Larne Lough to Islandmagee where he hid in a cave known today as 'Hill's Cave'.

Following the dismantling of the Bissett castle in Glenarm, Sir Randal McDonnell, a descendent of John Mor and Margery Bissett, began building the original part of the present Glenarm Castle some years prior to 1636. An inscription on the Barbican Gate into the castle reads : 'With the leave of God, this castle was built by Sir Randal MacDonnell, Knight, Erle of Antrim, having to his wife Dame Aellis O'Neill, in the year of Our Lord God, 1636'. Sir Randal had earlier made his peace with King James of England and was granted land which included all of the Glens of Antrim. In 1620 King James conferred on Sir Randal the title of Earl of Antrim. The castle has since been remodelled and restored and it is the seat of the present and 14th Earl, Lord Dunluce.

In the early 17th century the Earl of Antrim decided to plant his estate with lowland Scottish settlers of Presbyterian stock. Settlers such as the Donnelsons of Bay Farm, Carnlough, Sayers of Red Braes, Carnlough, Montgomerys and Dunns of Glenarm and the Shaws of Ballygally acquired land from the Earl and became important landlords in their own right. There were constant threats of rebellions by the native Irish against the settlers and in 1625

James Shaw of Ballygally erected a fortified house, Ballygally Castle, to shelter not only his family but also his servants and tenants. When the Irish rebellion of 1641 eventually took place the castle became a place of refuge for the settlers in that area. The fortified house still stands today and it is now an hotel.

In the 17th century regular imports of Scottish coal began arriving at Larne and the number of visitors from Scotland increased. In 1666 the historian Hollingshed referred to Larne harbour as being one of the chief havens of Ireland – in other words a safe and sheltered harbour. There is little doubt that the progress of Larne as an industrial town was due to its good harbour and its close position (a sea journey of less than 30 miles) to Britain.

In 18th century the exports from Larne included limestone, iron ore, potatoes, barley, oats and livestock. Due to religious discrimination and poor living conditions as well as oppression by some landlords many people, Presbyterians and Catholics alike, emigrated from this country to America. For many their chief point of embarkation was Larne and in 1717 the first direct sailing emigrant ship from Larne, 'Friend's Goodwill' carried 52 people to America in search of a new life. In the years 1771-1773 over 3000 emigrants embarked at Larne for the New World. The port also began to attract large quantities of flax and tobacco from America. Port development was slow however as horse-drawn carriages were the only form of land transport and even a small ship would take days to load and unload using baskets and wheelbarrows.

The oppression of the 18th century culminated in an uprising in 1798. Following the example of the French Revolution, where the poor peasant stock overthrew the rich aristocracy, Catholics in the south and mainly Presbyterians in the north rose in rebellion in an attempt to overthrow the establishment. The United Irishmen, as the rebels were called, started their northern campaign in Larne on

6th June when they attacked the local militia, the Tay Fencibles. Gathering forces from the neighbouring areas they marched 7000 strong towards the village of Antrim which was garrisoned by a company of yeomen and a troop of dragoons who supported the establishment. The following day rebels in the Cairncastle, Glenarm and Carnlough areas mustered at Bellair Hill outside the village of Glenarm in preparation for marching to Antrim. The 1800 strong crowd of men, woman and children were led by the local Presbyterian minister, Rev. Robert Acheson but before they could join their comrades they learned of the defeat of the rebels at Antrim and, faced with a hopeless situation, they were forced to disperse.

The early 19th century saw greater tolerance and resulted in a period of expansion and industrialisation. The building of the Antrim Coast Road in the 1830s from Larne to Ballycastle opened up the hitherto inaccessible Glens of Antrim to the public at large. The building of the Coast Road was a major feat of engineering by Scotsman William Bald who blasted the headlands so that the fallen rock would provide a stable foundation for the road which was to follow the coastline for much of its route. Enterprising men like Henry McNeill, who owned hotels in Larne, saw the possibilities of tourist trade to the Glens with their natural beauty and old world atmosphere. Thousands of tourists from Scotland and England flocked into Larne each summer to travel on horse-drawn carriages, supplied by McNeill, into the interior of the Glens. The Coast Road has had its problems over the years since it was built. Landslides down the steep slopes leading to the road have created havoc for travellers although most people see this as an irritant rather than a catastrophe. Near Glenarm clay slips have been a particular problem. After heavy rain the water seeps through the porous limestone structure and into the liassic clay below causing the clay to soften and slide down on to the road.

The Marchioness of Londonderry, a close relative of the Earl of Antrim, was the main landowner in Carnlough and much of the townscape of Carnlough was strongly influenced by her. As commercial life in the village progressed the Marchioness built a summer residence in 1848 at Garron Point (now St. MacNissi's co-educational Grammar School). The Londonderry Arms Hotel and a Town Hall in Carnlough were built by her in the 1850s. The Marchioness was largely responsible for the growth of the limestone industry in Carnlough which provided a source of employment. Bridges built across High Street and Harbour Road in 1854 allowed a railway to transport lime and limestone from the quarries behind Carnlough down to the harbour for export. The limestone bridges still dominate the view of the village of Carnlough today long after both the rail line and the limestone quarry closed down.

It was in the 1870s that a transatlantic service, run by 'State Line' began between Larne and America. A new quay was built and a steam crane erected. James Chaine, later the M.P. for Co. Antrim, bought Larne harbour in 1865 and developed it at great cost. The railway reached Larne in 1862 and for a short time a shipping service ran to Stranraer in Scotland. In 1872 a regular service to Stranraer was started using a specially built paddle steamer, 'Princess Louise'. The voyage took about 3 hours and though cattle were the main cargo, the boat carried 60 passengers a day. Chaine quickly realised that there was a serious disadvantage in not having a proper railway link with the centre of Co. Antrim. This was overcome in 1877 when Larne was connected with Ballymena by a narrow gauge line. Part of this line ran across the present Narrow Gauge Road near the junction of Point Street in Larne. This link may have been the reason why British Aluminium Co. built a smelter at Larne. Bauxite (the raw material used to make aluminium) and coal shipped in by the company made them Larne's biggest importers and the manufactured product was exported through Larne to Fort William in Scotland for finishing. The residue left by the

Aluminium Co. was dumped in special ponds in the area now known as the Redlands. James Chaine died in 1885 and a granite round tower (the Chaine Memorial) was erected near the harbour in 1888 by Belfast building contractor John Smith as recognition by the people of Larne of the great work Chaine had done in promoting the harbour and in opening rail links with Ballymena.

By 1914 there were clear possibilities of Home Rule being granted to Ireland and a parliament in Dublin. To northern Unionists this was unacceptable as it was a weakening of their link with Britain and the Ulster Volunteer Force was founded to protect the province from Home Rule. The Force needed weapons and Larne harbour was used to conduct a highly successful launching of arms. The event was the landing at Larne of 300 tons of rifles and ammunition during the night of 24th April 1914. The movement of these weapons sent a strong message to the British Government that Ulster Unionists would not tolerate any weakening of the union of Ireland and Britain or the cries of 'Home Rule' from Nationalists.

In 1912 the Chaine family sold the harbour to a group of local business men and the present Larne Harbour Ltd. was formed. The expansion of the port of Larne continued steadily and was given a major boost in 1947 when Colonel Frank Bustard started a 'roll on-roll off' (ro-ro) service which enabled lorries with their cargoes to drive straight on to the boats. From the 1950s Larne harbour developed into one of the best known container ports in Britain specialising in container services trading with cross-channel ports Stranraer, Cairnryan, Fleetwood and Preston. In 1976 a new elevated dual carriageway road to the harbour was completed and this allowed all heavy traffic bound for the harbour to move there quickly. In 1973 the harbour company became a subsidiary of European Ferries Group Plc. and since 1987 has been a member of the P&O Group.

Despite the success of the port the sea can be a cruel environment as was highlighted in 1953 when a short time after leaving Scotland the heavy seas burst open the stern doors of the car deck of the cross channel ferry, the 'Princess Victoria' en-route from Stranraer to Larne. The pressure of water was so great and the gates so badly buckled that orders were given to abandon ship when she began to sink near to the Copeland Islands off Donaghadee. Despite valiant efforts by the lifeboat service over 140 people, including locals from Larne, Glenarm and Carnlough, lost their lives, leaving the whole East Antrim area stunned as the news broke the following day.

The tragedy did not impede the tourist trade in Larne and the Glens of Antrim, which has continued unabated throughout this century and tourism is now a major source of revenue for the area. Other industries in the area have been less consistent than tourism. The closure of the GEC plant in 1991, a major employer in Larne, was a blow to the area. However as one business shrinks so others grow to fill the gap and F.G. Wilson's move to the GEC plant along with the establishment of a number of diverse smaller businesses, such as the salmon fishery at Glenarm, demonstrate the commercial attractions of the area with its capable workforce and excellent links to the mainland.

While industry provides much needed employment in the area it is in the tourism industry that many see the best opportunities for the future. It is thus important to retain the area's best natural resource, its landscape and architecture, and with this in mind both Glenarm and Carnlough have been designated Conservation Areas. Other tourism initiatives include Carnlough Harbour which has been substantially improved over recent years and the Tourist Information Centre in Larne which was officially opened in 1993. Set against one of the prettiest and most unspoilt landscapes in Europe, initiatives such as these should ensure that many new visitors will follow in the footsteps of those foreign visitors who, over the last 2000 years, have passed through Larne, the 'Gateway to the Glens'.

Important Historical Dates

c.3000 B.C.   First settlers in the Larne area.

c.100 B.C.   Lathar, son of Hugony the Great, King of Ireland, is granted a territory along the Antrim Coast, the name of which was later corrupted to 'Larne'.

205 A.D.   Roman Emperor Serverus refers to Larne Lough and its natural advantages.

517   Birth of St. Comgall at Magheramorne.

1018   Battle at Larne Lough between Viking chief, Einar Jarl, and Konofogor (Connor), King of Ireland.

c.1200   Glenarm granted a charter by King John making it perhaps the oldest town in Ulster.

c.1250   Building of Olderfleet Castle, Larne.

1315   Edward Bruce and his army of 6000 men land at Larne in an attempt to conquer Ireland.

1470   Founding of a Franciscan monastery in Glenarm.

1625   Ballygally 'Castle' built by Scottish planter, James Shaw, as a fortified house.

1636   Building of second Glenarm Castle completed.

1668   First Presbyterian 'Head of the Town' church built.

1752   First slated roof in Larne, at Dunluce Street.

1760   Building begins on St. Patrick's Church of Ireland Church, Glenarm.

1771   John Wesley preaches at No.9 Main St, Larne.

1798   United Irishmen begin hostilities in Larne.

1832	William Bald oversees the construction of the Antrim Coast Road.
1848	Garron Tower is erected for the Marchioness of Londonderry as a summer residence.
1854	Limestone bridges and rail line constructed in Carnlough.
1869	McGarel Town Hall, Larne, built at the junction of Main Street and Cross Street.
1870s	Regular ferry service established between Larne and Stranraer.
1877	Narrow gauge railway from the harbour at Larne to Ballymena established.
1888	Replica round tower built in memory of James Chaine who owned Larne Harbour.
1892	Larne, first town in N. Ireland to have electricity.
1914	Ulster Volunteer Force lands arms at Larne Harbour.
1938	Borough Charter awarded to Larne.
1953	Princess Victoria disaster.
1976	Harbour Highway links Larne Harbour with the main road to Belfast.
1978	Glenarm is designated a Conservation Area.
1981	Carnlough is designated a Conservation Area.
1993	Tourist Information Centre opened in Larne.
1994	Moyle Hospital, Larne, closes and patients are transferred to Area Hospital at Antrim.

Name and Address

Telephone

LARNE TOWN HALL

The Town Hall was built in 1869 at a cost of nearly £6000 provided by the late Charles McGarel whose residence had been at Magheramorne House. On the site of the Town Hall had been an old stagecoach inn which was demolished to make way for the new building. Charles McGarel, originally from Hungry Hill, Raloo, bestowed to Larne not only the Town Hall but the McGarel Cemetery. Charles died childless in 1876 (the same year as the well known Town Hall clock was installed). His estate at Glynn was bequeathed to his wife's brother, Sir James Hogg, an ancestor of the present-day Lord Hailsham, Quentin Hogg.

With thanks to Craig's Cellars

B

Name and Address	Telephone

HIGH STREET, CARNLOUGH

High Street in Carnlough was once the main thoroughfare in the village, being part of the old coastal route before the coming of the Coast Road in the 1830s. As the new road took a straighter route closer to the harbour it claimed most of the Glens bound traffic and High Street became known as Back Street. The dominant feature of the street is a limestone bridge which was erected by the Marquis and Marchioness of Londonderry in 1853-4 to enable limestone to be transported by rail from the quarries behind the village down to the harbour where it was loaded on ships and exported to England and Scotland for use as flux for the iron and steel industry.

With thanks to McCormick Bros.

Name and Address	Telephone

THE PATH

The Path is part of an old roadway which was the main route from Larne to Glenarm prior to the building of the Coast Road in the 1830s. It is a very steep hill and the roadway winds its way upwards in an attempt to make access easier for the stage-coaches which used to pass this way to Glenarm Castle and beyond. The horses pulling the stage-coaches often had great difficulty in climbing the Path and trace horses were used to help them up the steep incline. The stables at the foot of the hill where these trace horses were kept can still be seen. Further up the Path the land drops perilously towards the sea and over the centuries several horsemen have fallen to their deaths on the seaward side of the road.

With thanks to Coach House Antiques

Name and Address	_Telephone_

ALTMORE STREET PRESBYTERIAN CHURCH

Up until 1829 all Presbyterians in Glenarm worshipped in the old Presbyterian church near Cloney. In that year a 'split' occurred when Rev. Alexander Montgomery and his followers broke away from the general body. As his 101 seat-holders had a majority they remained in the old church and the 50 who continued to subscribe to the Westminster Confession had to find a new building to worship in. For some time they had to worship in the open air but eventually new premises were built at the head of Altmore Street. This new church was opened on July 12, 1835 for the Subscribing Presbyterians.

Name and Address	*Telephone*

St. Patrick's Church, Glenarm

One of Glenarm's most familiar landmarks, St. Patrick's was built in the 1760s beside the ruins of a 15th century Franciscan monastery whose walls provided stones for the new church. It is the earliest known example of a church being built in Gothic style in Ireland. Some of the church's windows were altered in the 19th century but the original windows survive on the tower and on the wall beside it. Another 18th century relic in the church is a window in the old Antrim pew dedicated to 'Milesius, King of Spain', a semi-mythical king who led the Celts on their last invasion of Ireland. A new spire was erected in 1823 when repairs costing £1200 were made to the church.

Name and Address	Telephone

OLDERFLEET CASTLE

The castle at Olderfleet is said to have built by a Scottish family called Bissett who settled in Glenarm in the 13th century, although other sources suggest that it was built by the Vikings or Danes and only later occupied by the Bissetts. Close to the castle in 1018 a famous battle between the Vikings and the local clan took place in the Bay of Ulpeksfiord, the name given to Larne Lough by the Vikings. A skeleton, believed to be of a soldier who fought in this battle was unearthed on the shore at Larne in 1840. The castle has lain in ruins for many years at Curran Point although its designation as an ancient monument should now ensure that further deterioration will not take place.

With thanks to Larne Borough Council

Name and Address	Telephone

LARNE HARBOUR

The natural advantages of depth and shelter which Larne Lough possessed were known to early Greeks and Romans between the 2nd and 3rd centuries and in succeeding centuries to the Vikings and the Scots. In the 18th century the town harbour at the bottom of Quay Lane was the chief exit point for 3000 emigrants bound for America. It was James Chaine in the mid 19th century who developed the present harbour and established a link with Stranraer. In 1846 Captain George Adams of the Royal Navy reported that Larne Harbour was 'the safest and easiest of access of any port on the north-east coast of Ireland'. Today Larne is an important container port and Ulster's busiest ferry port.

With thanks to P&O European Ferries

Name and Address	Telephone

MEETING HOUSE, CAIRNCASTLE

This hamlet at the junction of five roads can boast a public house and two churches or meeting houses, hence the origin of the name. The public house has been in the hands of the Moore family for many generations and was named 'Meetinghouse' which led a local resident to joke that everyone could meet at Meetinghouse in the same 'spirit'. The origin of the townland name of Cairncastle comes from a cairn of rocks at the edge of Ballygally Head on which stood a 'castle' many centuries ago. One of the Presbyterian meeting houses, which had been built in 1668, was taken down recently and a new church was erected in its place.

With thanks to Meetinghouse

I

Name and Address	Telephone

CARNEGIE LIBRARY

Scottish-born, American millionaire and philanthropist, Andrew Carnegie, helped build and equip 2500 libraries around the world including the red-brick building at the corner of Thorndale Avenue and Victoria Road, Larne. The Carnegie Library was officially opened in 1905 and served the people of Larne and district for 75 years. In 1980 a more modern library was erected in Pound Street and the Carnegie Building was vacated. Some time later the Larne and District Historical Society took over the building as an historical centre and museum. Victoria Road was constructed in 1900-01 linking the old Fairhill with Clonlee. It was originally known as Victoria Street.

With thanks to Pollock Jewellers

Name and Address	Telephone

ST. CEDMA'S CHURCH

St. Cedma is said to be a corruption of Setna who was the father of St. Comgall of Magheramorne. The parish church of Larne and Inver, St. Cedma's, stands on the site of an early 6th century Augustinian Friary and is now at the centre of what used to be three separate Christian foundations – Inverbeg, Invermore and Drumalis. The rectors of this church between 1609 and 1839 were also the Deans of Connor. One of these was the Rev. G. W. Storey, who was a chaplain in the army of William III, Prince of Orange. An interesting feature is that called 'the Leper Window' where it is said lepers used to watch and listen from outside the church.

Name and Address	Telephone

BALLYGALLY HEAD

This rugged headland is the remains of a vent of one of the ancient volcanoes from which lavas poured out all over Co. Antrim 60 million years ago, cooling to become basalt rock. When the volcanic activity ceased the molten lava cooled inside the vent to become a hard plug of basalt which today stands out from the softer rocks which have been eroded around it. The molten lava lay on top of a chalk or limestone layer. Along the coast at Carnlough and Glenarm part of the upper basaltic layers have been eroded over the millennia to expose the underlying rocks giving rise to the extensive limestone quarrying industry which has long existed in this area.

With thanks to Book Nook

Name and Address	Telephone

CASTLE STREET AND THE BARBICAN GATE

The bridge in Castle Street across Glenarm River at the Barbican Gate was built in 1682 and this road used to be known as Bridge Street. The bridge leads to Glenarm Castle, built by the first Earl of Antrim as an inscribed stone on the barbican states : 'With the leave of God, this castle was built by Sir Randal MacDonnell, Knight, Erle of Antrim, having to his wife Dame Aellis O'Neill, in the Year of our Lord God, 1636'. One evening in 1754 the local Minister, Thomas Brown, dined with the 5th Earl of Antrim and, after some refreshments, left by the Barbican Gate. Unfortunately in the darkness he missed his footing, fell over the edge of the low bridge and was drowned.

With thanks to Scullion's Newsagents

- SAM MCLARNON -

Name and Address	Telephone

CARNLOUGH HARBOUR

At the turn of the 18th and 19th centuries a loose stone pier was constructed here for the first time by a local landowner called Phil Gibbons and in the mid 19th century a second pier was built. This was to ensure that limestone brought down on the railway from the quarries above the village could be easily loaded on to boats. This harbour did a flourishing trade with ports in Scotland and England for many years. Following the closure of the limestone quarries the harbour came to cater for pleasure boats and local fishing boats. Recent regeneration with investment from the International Fund for Ireland has helped to give this scenic little harbour a welcome boost.

With thanks to B.P. Killough

- Sam McLARNON -

Name and Address	Telephone

BRIDGE END TAVERN

The warm and relaxed welcome which greets today's visitor to the Bridge End Tavern is a far cry from the dark days of early September 1854. A visitor to the Glenarm Fair who stayed at the tavern did not travel alone but had brought with her the dreaded cholera. By the time her death was reported on the evening of the Fair day many Fair goers had been exposed to the infection. The Tavern and those who attended it were strictly quarantined causing the outbreak to die out after a week, but it was too late for the landlord and his family who, along with a number of locals and visitors, soon perished from the disease and were buried in a single mass grave beside St. Patrick's Church.

With thanks to the Bridge End Tavern

Name and Address

Telephone

GLENO

Just a short drive off the shore road from Larne to Carrickfergus, Gleno is a quaint and picturesque little village at the head of the Gleno valley. One of Gleno's best known natural features is its waterfall which was taken over by the National Trust in 1970 and attracts many tourists each year. Visitors can also sample the village's home-made ice-cream at 'Maud's Ice-Cream Dairy'. On the wall of the ice-cream factory is a blue plaque in honour of Theodore Roosevelt, US President from 1901-1909, whose ancestors were said to come from the Carneal area near Gleno.

With thanks to Shek Hair Group

Name and Address	*Telephone*

LARGY CHURCH

Prior to 1841 the people of Ardclinis and Carnlough did not have a place to worship since their old Ardclinis church had fallen into ruin. For a time divine service in the area according to the rites of the Church of Ireland was performed in a barn and later in the Turnly schoolhouse at Drumnasole. In 1836 Ardclinis became a parish in its own right with its own resident rector. John Wilson, who lived at Harphall House became the first rector. Some time later work began on the building of a church at the Largy on the old coast road. St. Mary's Church was opened on July 19, 1841.

Name and Address	Telephone

GLENARM GLEN

Much of the glen of Glenarm is owned by the 14th Earl of Antrim, Lord Dunluce. The steeper slopes on either side of the glen are forested while the flatter valley floor provides ideal grazing land. A large area of the glen is known as Deerpark, referring to a time in previous centuries when the Earl of Antrim grazed reindeer in the valley. The antlers shed by the deer each year were often picked up by local tenants and when pushed into holes in their cottage walls provided useful coat hangers. The Glenarm River running down through the centre of the estate is well stocked with salmon. In 1988 the Northern Salmon Co. Ltd. set up a freshwater hatchery for breeding fish in the river.

With thanks to Millbrook Supplies

Name and Address	Telephone

DRUMALIS

Drumalis, 'the round hill with the fort', was once the site of a 13th century Premonstratensian friary. The 'White Canons', as the monks were known, lived here for 300 years until their land was forfeited to the Crown in 1591, following the dissolution of the monasteries in 1542 by Henry VIII. Drumalis was owned by a number of families before being associated with the Agnew family of Kilwaughter in the early 19th century. In the late 19th century it was sold to James Chaine, M.P. who erected a private dwelling house here. The property was purchased by the Cross and Passion Order of nuns in 1930 and Chaine's residence is now a convent retreat house.

Name and Address	Telephone

THE BLACK ARCH

This basalt arch was built in the 1830s by the workers who constructed the Coast Road. This great engineering feat was supervised by Scot, William Bald. He devised a means of blasting the cliff so that the huge rocks rested at the water's edge creating a foundation for the road. When completed it was called the 'Grand Military Highway' reflecting its primary purpose to ensure that all of the country was accessible to the forces of law and order. In the late 19th century Henry McNeill, a Larne hotelier, used it to transport thousands of tourists from Scotland and England in horse-drawn (later motorised) transport along the Coast Road into the heart of the Glens area.

With thanks to Mr R. Alexander of Curtains Plus

Name and Address	Telephone

APSLEY'S, MAIN STREET

In 1903 James Boyd, newsagent, family goods and souvenir retailer, sold this shop to S. & L. Apsley. It remained in the Apsley family until 1990 when it was sold to Mr Bobby Lyttle. This well-known shop has retained the traditional style of facade which would have been common in Larne in the early part of this century. Next door on the wall of Bobby Lyttle's menswear shop, there is a plaque commemorating the fact that John Wesley, the 'Father of Methodism', visited here in 1771. On the 4th July of that year he preached from the first floor window of this building to a large crowd which had gathered in the street.

With thanks to Apsley's

- Sam McLarnon -

T

Name and Address	*Telephone*

CHAINE MEMORIAL TOWER

This tower was constructed in 1888 in memory of one of Larne's most influential businessmen, James Chaine. He saw the natural advantages of Larne Lough and invested large sums of money to develop the port of Larne. He was also instrumental in securing a steam service in 1872 between Larne and Stranraer. In 1885 while presenting an address to the Prince of Wales at Larne Harbour he sustained a chill and died a short time later of pneumonia. The people of Larne wanted to erect a monument to the man who had helped the development of their town. It was decided to build a 92 ft. high tower resembling the ancient Irish round tower at Antrim, the birthplace of Chaine.

With thanks to East Antrim Electrical

Name and Address	Telephone

STRAIDKILLY

The little hamlet of Straidkilly, about a quarter of a mile north of Glenarm, is often referred to as the 'slipping village'. It sits on a platform of limestone or chalk which is subsiding due to the fact that it rests on a thin layer of lias clay. When heavy rain falls the water percolates through the limestone down into the clay making it very soft. The heavier limestone above and the buildings on it sink downwards, thus creating the idea of a 'slipping village'. The soft clay squeezed down by the limestone often slips down on to the Coast Road causing it to be blocked. During the last century workmen known as 'slipmen' were employed to shift the clay with shovels and wheelbarrows.

With thanks to T.H. O'Kane Sales

Name and Address	Telephone

FEYSTOWN CHURCH

St. Mary's Catholic Church at Feystown, 4 miles south of Glenarm village, was built in 1828 to replace a much smaller church built 18 years earlier a few hundred yards away in the hillside. Inset in the altar rails of the church is a replica in glass of a famous 9th century bishop's crozier which once rested in the chancel window of the old Ardclinis Church, situated between Garron Point and Glenariffe. The crozier was sold to Dublin Museum in 1962 and the money was donated to the parish to defer the cost of extensive renovations. On the southward gable wall of the church looking out towards Slemish is a statue of St. Patrick, the work of the late Countess of Antrim.

Name and Address	*Telephone*

ST. PATRICK'S CHURCH, CAIRNCASTLE

St. Patrick's Church of Ireland Church in Cairncastle was erected in 1815 and stands close to the site of a much older church, some remains of which can still be seen in the churchyard. In the graveyard adjoining the present church is an old gnarled Spanish Chestnut tree. Following the defeat of the Spanish Armada in 1588, a number of galleons foundered on the north coast of Ulster. An oral tradition in the area states that a body from one of the boats was washed up in Ballygally Bay and the remains were buried in the graveyard of the old church at Cairncastle. In the pocket of the dead man were seeds of a chestnut tree from which the present tree is said to have sprung.

- sam MacLARNON -

Name and Address	*Telephone*

GLYNN

This picturesque village, named after the Gaelic 'Glynn' meaning 'river' is situated along the shore road south of Larne. Many of the houses in the village had thatched roofs until a few years ago. In the graveyard surrounding St. John's Parish Church are ruins of an old church which apparently was situated on the same site as an earlier church founded by St. Patrick in the 5th century. A cross here was said to mark the most southerly extent of the first Earl of Antrim's territory in the early 17th century – 'from the Cutts of Coleraine to the Curran of Larne'. The War Memorial was unveiled in November 1921 to commemorate those soldiers who lost their lives in World War I.

With thanks to Frames Unlimited

Name and Address	Telephone

GLENCLOY

The origin of the name of this glen is clouded in mystery. It has been suggested that it means 'the glen of the fences' or 'the glen of the sword'. Like the other eight glens it is a glaciated valley carved out by rivers of ice at the end of the Ice Age. These giant glaciers moved across the land leaving behind a glen whose shape has probably changed little in the 10 000 years since then apart from changes wrought by man. Early hunters and the farming communities who followed, cleared the dense forest-clad slopes of the glen and today the bare hillsides of Glencloy show the scars of the flourishing limestone industry which existed for over a century.

With thanks to McKillop's

Name and Address	Telephone

THE VENNEL

This little narrow winding street was once the main thoroughfare into Glenarm prior to the building of the Coast Road in the 1830's. In earlier days it was known as Larne Street, being the main road leading to that town. It was built along the path of an old Anglo-Norman road which linked the old castle in the village to the De Courcy castle at Carrickfergus. Many of these old roads were made over headlands and into valleys and as a result were steep and very muddy in wet weather making the transporting of horse-drawn coaches very difficult. The Vennel lost much of its traffic after the Coast Road was built and is now generally only used by those living there.

With thanks to McAuley's

Local Directory
and Sponsors

We would like to express our thanks to the
following businesses and organisations
without whose help and support this book
would not have been possible.

Carnlough (STD code 01574)

	Tel	Fax
Grocer MCCORMICK BROTHERS 22-24 HIGH STREET	885185	
Pharmacy B. P. KILLOUGH 19/21 MARINE ROAD	885441	
Confectionery & Fancy Goods MCKILLOP'S 16 HARBOUR ROAD	885236	

Glenarm (STD code 01574)

	Tel	Fax
Antiques and Paint Stripping COACH HOUSE ANTIQUES 66 DICKEYSTOWN ROAD	841022	
Auctioneers, Valuers and Estate Agency O'KANES OF GLENARM 22 TOBERWINE STREET	841470	841469
Butcher MCAULEY 11 TOBERWINE STREET	841249	
Newsagents, Tobacconist, Local Maps & Guides SCULLIONS NEWSAGENTS 32-34 TOBERWINE STREET	841293	
Public House BRIDGE END TAVERN 1-3 TOBERWINE STREET	841252	

Larne (STD code 01574)

	Tel	Fax
Bar & Off Licence CRAIGS CELLARS 15 MAIN STREET	272861	
Bookshop, Newsagent and Post Office BOOK NOOK 96 MAIN STREET	260395	260395

Larne (STD code 01574)

	Tel	Fax
Electrical Goods		
EAST ANTRIM ELECTRICAL		
71 MAIN STREET	260468	
Ferry Operator		
P & O EUROPEAN FERRIES		
THE HARBOUR	274400	270949
Framer		
FRAMES UNLIMITED		
20 MAIN ROAD, GLYNN	275688	
Garden Machinery Sales, Tool and Plant Hire		
MILLBROOK SUPPLIES		
4 BROWNDOD ROAD	273967	279859
5 Murrayfield Shopping Centre	260057	
Hairdresser – Ladies and Gents		
SHEK HAIR GROUP		
67 MAIN STREET	272353	
Home Furnishings, Interior Design & Wall Coverings		
CURTAINS PLUS BY ALEXANDER		
28 POINT STREET	277755	272733
Jeweller		
POLLOCK JEWELLERS		
60 MAIN STREET	260017	
Local Government		
LARNE BOROUGH COUNCIL		
VICTORIA ROAD	272313	260660
Menswear		
BOBBY LYTTLE MENSWEAR		
7-9 MAIN STREET	260817	270764
Newsagents, Souvenirs		
APSLEY'S		
11-13 MAIN STREET	260510	270764
Public House & Restaurant		
MEETINGHOUSE		
120 BRUSTIN BRAE ROAD, CAIRNCASTLE	583252	

Open Diary

This section is provided to record personal
dates such as birthdays, anniversaries and
other important annual events.

January

1
....

2
....

3
....

4
....

5
....

6
....

7
....

8
....

9
....

10
....

11
....

12
....

13
....

14
....

15
....

16
....

17
....

18
....

19
....

20
....

21
....

22
....

23
....

24
....

25
....

26
....

27
....

28
....

29
....

30
....

31
....

February

1	16
2	17
3	18
4	19
5	20
6	21
7	22
8	23
9	24
10	25
11	26
12	27
13	28
14	29
15	

March

1	16
2	17
3	18
4	19
5	20
6	21
7	22
8	23
9	24
10	25
11	26
12	27
13	28
14	29
15	30
	31

April

1	*16*
2	*17*
3	*18*
4	*19*
5	*20*
6	*21*
7	*22*
8	*23*
9	*24*
10	*25*
11	*26*
12	*27*
13	*28*
14	*29*
15	*30*

May

1	16
2	17
3	18
4	19
5	20
6	21
7	22
8	23
9	24
10	25
11	26
12	27
13	28
14	29
15	30
	31

June

1

2

3

4

5

6

7

8

9

10

11

12

13

14

15

16

17

18

19

20

21

22

23

24

25

26

27

28

29

30

July

1	16
2	17
3	18
4	19
5	20
6	21
7	22
8	23
9	24
10	25
11	26
12	27
13	28
14	29
15	30
	31

August

1 ....

2 ....

3 ....

4 ....

5 ....

6 ....

7 ....

8 ....

9 ....

10 ....

11 ....

12 ....

13 ....

14 ....

15 ....

16 ....

17 ....

18 ....

19 ....

20 ....

21 ....

22 ....

23 ....

24 ....

25 ....

26 ....

27 ....

28 ....

29 ....

30 ....

31 ....

September

1	16
2	17
3	18
4	19
5	20
6	21
7	22
8	23
9	24
10	25
11	26
12	27
13	28
14	29
15	30

October

1	16
2	17
3	18
4	19
5	20
6	21
7	22
8	23
9	24
10	25
11	26
12	27
13	28
14	29
15	30
	31

November

1	*16*
2	*17*
3	*18*
4	*19*
5	*20*
6	*21*
7	*22*
8	*23*
9	*24*
10	*25*
11	*26*
12	*27*
13	*28*
14	*29*
15	*30*

December

1	16
2	17
3	18
4	19
5	20
6	21
7	22
8	23
9	24
10	25
11	26
12	27
13	28
14	29
15	30
	31

Cottage

Publications

Dear Reader

We hope you have found this book both enjoyable and useful. If you feel that it could have been improved in any way do please let us know.

This book is one of our 'Illustrated History and Companion' range. Other towns and areas currently featured in this range include:–

Ballycastle and the Heart of the Glens
Ballymena
Ballymoney
Bangor
City of Derry
Coleraine and the Causeway Coast
Donaghadee
Hillsborough
Holywood
Newtownards

If you require more information call us on 01247 883876 or write to:– **Cottage Publications**
15 Ballyhay Road
Donaghadee, Co. Down
N. Ireland
BT21 0NG

Timothy S Johnston